27 CLUB

PARANORMAL

COINCIDENCES

27 CLUB—PARANORMAL COINCIDENCES

LEGAL NOTICE:

This book is copyright protected. It is only for personal use. This book cannot be distributed, sold, used, reproduced, quoted, amended, or paraphrased in part or in whole, without the written consent of the author.

DISCLAIMER NOTICE:

The information contained within this manuscript is for educational and entertainment purposes only. Efforts have been made to present accurate, timely, and reliable information. However, by reading this manuscript, the reader agrees that under no circumstance is the author or publisher responsible for any losses of any type that are incurred as a result of the use of any information, or the experiencing of any information contained within this manuscript; this includes, but is not limited to errors, omissions, or inaccuracies. Readers acknowledge the author has made no attempt to offer medical, legal, professional, or financial advice. Readers agree that information presented is for purposes of fostering conversation and curiosity. Readers agree to immediately seek assistance via well-established crisis intervention resources and/or a duly licensed professional(s) for any idea of self-harm, confrontation, or harm to others. The content within this book has been derived from multiple sources. No warranties of any kind are expressed, declared, or implied.

PREFACE

If the only 27 CLUB Superstar commonalities were a name with a probable "J" at the beginning, and death at the age of 27, there would be noteworthiness. Obviously, these factors are what brought the phenomenon of a 27 CLUB into existence. At face value, this is enough for many people to "buy in," while others will dismiss the notion as mere coincidence.

Astonishingly, the existence of dozens of additional striking patterns begs the question, is there really more to this than meets the eye? From calendar concentrations of time and events to Woodstock, the Zodiac, and multiple additional categories, how much of the 27 CLUB is simply coincidence and how much points to some form of manipulation by an outside force?

Most significant events and experiences leading to the deaths of Brian Jones, Jimi Hendrix, Janis Joplin, Jim Morrison, Kurt Cobain, and Amy Winehouse are already well documented. Exploration into the unique ways 27 CLUB members intertwine is mostly uncharted territory. Does it seem to be a coincidence that beginning letters of their cities of death spell "PARALLELS?" And that there is a strong concentration of latitudes (another name for parallels) for their locations of death? Or that three of the six most recognized 27 CLUB members were 9 years old when their parents divorced? And those combined ages total 27? Or how all these superstars died near western boundaries of two continents. Or that their deaths occur in close proximity to the Equinoxes and a single Solstice? These barely scratch the surface of what exceeds coincidence.

With abundant information to consider, both right-brained and left-brained people will enjoy the optional approaches into this information odyssey. Tables of information alternate with pages of more detailed explanations, with an effort to minimize impertinent verbiage. Occasional four-line lyrics are interspersed throughout, offering an artistic vantagepoint from which to speculate over possible causes and associations. One can browse highlights or look further in depth. The book can be a 2-hour read, or the subject matter of energizing discussions over coffee for months. How could there be so many interrelated patterns?

Continued analysis would cause a perpetual publication delay as new angles emerge. Compelling content will fuel the additional surfacing of 27 CLUB variables and comparison with other groups.

Superstar CLUB membership may be closed. Hopefully, it concluded with Amy Winehouse. Only time will tell. A potentially eligible candidate is referenced near the end of the book to demonstrate how patterns could be used to aid in determining vulnerability and possibly avoiding new accessions. Cobain's death is generally accepted as a suicide. Helpline contact numbers are believed to be correct and current at the time of submission. Optimistically, no more 27s die.

Please enjoy a journey into the stunning interrelatedness of the 27 CLUB!

CONTENTS

NATIONAL SUICIDE PREVENTION LIFELINE

1-800-273-8255

NATIONAL de PREVENCION del SUICIDIO
1-888-628-9454

VETERANS CRISIS LINE
1-800-273-8255
Or TEXT 838255

DISASTER DISTRESS HELPLINE
1-800-985-5990
Or TEXT 1-800-985-5990

27 CLUB--PARANORMAL COINCIDENCES

Janis Joplin, Jimi Hendrix, Jim Morrison, Brian Jones, Kurt Cobain, Amy Winehouse. These are the biggest names of the 27 CLUB. They were all extremely popular music performers who would not live beyond the age of 27.

Passing away at the age of 27 and being famous performers is only one thread of the much broader tapestry of commonalities within the 27 CLUB. The letter "J" is common to the CORE FOUR (Brian "J"ones, "J"imi Hendrix, "J"anis "J"oplin, and "J"im Morrison), who all died between "J"uly 3, 1969, and "J"uly 3, 1971, the same date otherwise expressed as 7/3 and all within a 730 day, 2-year period.

7/3/69

Brian Jones

Jimi Hendrix

Janis Joplin

Jim Morrison

7/3/71

730 DAYS

DATES OF DEATH

MEMBER	MONTH/DAY	YEAR
BRIAN JONES	JUL 3	1969
JIMI HENDRIX	SEP 18	1970
JANIS JOPLIN	OCT 4	1970
JIM MORRISON	JUL 3	1971
KURT COBAIN	APR 5	1994
AMY WINEHOUSE	JUL 23	2011

THE CORE FOUR

JONES	DIED	7/3	1969
HENDRIX	DIED	9/18	1970
JOPLIN	DIED	10/4	1970
MORRISON	DIED	7/3	1971

27th CALENDAR WEEK OF 1969, JONES DIES

27th CALENDAR WEEK OF 1971, MORRISON DIES

27th DAY OF NOVEMBER 1942, HENDRIX IS BORN

27 DAYS BEFORE HALLOWEEN, JOPLIN DIES

7/3 - MONTH/DAY JONES AND MORRISON DIED

730 - DAYS IN THE 2 YEARS OF CORE FOUR
  DEATHS

$$(365 + 365 = 730)$$

Add Amy "J"ade Winehouse and Kurt Cobain, and you have the BIG SIX. The only member without a "J," Cobain's "K" immediately follows "J" in the alphabet. He is further distinguished as the only one of the BIG SIX to die in the first half of his final calendar year, with the other five passing away during the second half of their years. The letter, "H" is the consonant that immediately precedes "J" in the alphabet. "H" marks the beginning letter of words designating the settings of death for all BIG SIX. In addition, many less well known 27 CLUB member's death settings range from "H"illsides to "H"ighways. Three of the BIG SIX (CORE FOUR plus Cobain and Winehouse) died in cities that begin with "L."

"H, J, K, L" is a string of sequential consonants with exceptionally strong significance for the 27 CLUB.

H, J, K, L

HENDRIX COINCIDENCES

BORN ON THE 27th OF NOVEMBER

BIRTH DATE 11/27/1942: 1+1+2+7+1+9+4+2 = 27

DEATH MONTH + DEATH DAY = AGE AT DEATH

$$9 + 18 = 27$$

SUM OF BIRTHDAY AND DEATH DAY DIGITS = BIRTH YEAR

$$1+1+2+7+4+2 \quad + \quad 9+1+8+7+0 = '42$$

DAY OF MONTH + YEAR BORN = YEAR JONES DIED;

$$27 + '42 = '69$$

DAYS MISSED FROM 27th YEAR = '69, YEAR JONES DIED

BORN AND DIED ON SAME WEEKDAY (FRIDAYS)

PLAYED WOODSTOCK AND MONTEREY POP, LIKE JOPLIN

DIED 13 MONTHS TO THE DAY AFTER WOODSTOCK

BORN IN THE SAME STATE AS COBAIN…WASHINGTON

DIED IN THE SAME CITY AS WINEHOUSE…LONDON

"27" returns repeatedly in the lives of the BIG SIX. Jimi Hendrix's birthday is November 27th. Halloween is 27 days after the anniversary of Janis Joplin's death on October 4th. Amy Winehouse was born when her mother was 27. Brian Jones and Jim Morrison passed away during the 27th calendar week of their respective death years. Not only did Kurt Cobain depart from his wife at the age of 27, but so did two of his wife's former bandmates.

The notorious number "13" surfaces a number of times in their lives. One of multiple examples is that Jimi Hendrix died exactly 13 months from the final day of Woodstock. "Lucky 7" was not lucky for Jones, Morrison, or Winehouse who all passed away during the 7th month ("J"uly), of their final years.

When Jim Morrison died on the very same day Brian Jones passed away two years previously, speculation intensified over this intriguing pattern with Jimi Hendrix's and Janis Joplin's deaths situated between the two. It would be 23 years later when Kurt Cobain died, adding a refueling of speculation regarding the pattern of 27-year-old Superstar deaths. After 17 more years, Amy Winehouse would provide a resurgence of the same speculation.

REPETITIVE CLUB NUMBERS

FROM: "TWENTY SEVENDING" © 2013

"Scattered 'round the world, cities were mangled
From the ashes of a war, stars were spangled
Growing into steel from the remains of rust
Rose to the top on an incredible gust"

Additional links to the number 27 only hint at the volume of 27 CLUB coincidences. There are multiple other significant numbers as well. Beginning letters of certain words are abnormally present. Add map coordinates of births and deaths. Specific weekdays, seasons, and calendar concentrations are apparent. Zodiac patterns surface. Links to celestial events materialize. Associations with military conflicts come into focus. Commonalities between the Monterey Pop Festival in 1967 and Woodstock in 1969 emerge. Nationality, gender, and prime-number-associated patterns of death begin to crystallize, among others.

We are left to wonder what greater and/or continued accomplishments might be associated with these extremely popular performers, had they lived on. Would living beyond the age of 27 have produced additional memorable hits and tours? Would they have stayed true to their original styles of music, or would they have morphed into something recognizably different? Would they have overshadowed those who succeeded in their physical absence? What other courses would have been affected? We will never really know.

PATTERNS

<u>FROM: "TWENTY SEVENDING"</u> © 2013

"Growing up brought the pains, that growing up brings
Cramping thumbs practiced, on a neck of six strings
Like the astronaut, that started with a kite
On the whim of maybe, you started the flight"

People are attracted to stars. Brilliant objects in the heavens...
Brilliant performers on stage. We marvel. We succumb to curiosity.
We look forward to the next encounter. We are captivated by the
phenomenon.   Looking for patterns is a component of human nature.
Patterns, whether a result of cause or coincidence, are much like
beauty...they exist in the eye of the beholder. Is there a direction in
which you are pulled? How much coincidence is required before it
morphs into probable cause-and-effect?

The relationship between coincidental occurrences has been formally
studied since at least the 1700s and has involved some of the greater
minds of their times. Perhaps the most famous is Carl Jung who
popularized the concept of "synchronicity." Others brought forth the
terms, serendipity, seriality, and simulpathity. And somehow, this
collection of words referencing coincidence falls into the coincidental
pattern of all beginning with the letter, "S."

Fans continue to mourn the deaths of these exceptionally talented
Superstars. Birthdays of the BIG SIX are celebrated in articles, on
social media, and at in-person events. On the anniversaries of their
deaths, fans continue to pay homage. Jim Morrison's grave in Paris is
the endpoint of pilgrimages by fans, young and old, where reports of
a ghost have surfaced. Some even "party" there with Jim.

Death is terribly tragic. But coincidence captures curiosity.

STARS

JONES COINCIDENCES

JONES BORN IN '42; BIG SIX DEATHS OCCURRED OVER 42 YEARS.

      JONES ('69) UNTIL WINEHOUSE ('11) IS 42 YEARS

JONES MARKED THE BEGINNING OF ALL BIG SIX DEATHS

DIED 27TH CALENDAR WEEK OF YEAR LIKE MORRISON

DAY OF MONTH + YEAR JONES WAS BORN IS '70, WHICH IS THE YEAR HENDRIX AND JOPLIN DIED

$$28 + '42 = '70$$

AVERAGE DISTANCE BETWEEN BIG SIX BIRTHPLACES AND LOCATION OF DEATH IS 1,864 MILES. DIVIDED BY JONES '69 YEAR OF DEATH = 27

69 MILES IS THE DISTANCE OF 1 DEGREE OF LATITUDE

DIED AT 0 DEGREE MERIDIAN LIKE HENDRIX/WINEHOUSE

LIVED LESS THAN 10,000 DAYS LIKE COBAIN

DIED AT COTCHFORD FARM, THE SETTING INSPIRATION FOR "WINNIE THE POOH"

"27" is an abstract representation of quantity. We frequently use numbers in our daily lives, often without even realizing. What time is it? What is today's date? I need to phone a friend. I need to enter my Personal Identification Number (PIN). Which checkout aisle is open? Which highway should I take and what is the speed limit? We even assign numbers to quality...Is that a 4-star hotel?

The 13th floor may represent more than just quantity. "13" is generally considered to be an unlucky number while "7" is considered to foster luck. Some choose to ascribe luck to more personalized numbers, such as, "5 is my lucky number!" Is luck simply a "happy coincidence," or could there be other factors at play? Is bad luck an "unhappy coincidence," or a cause-and-effect situation? Numbers can alter moods and attitudes in this way.

As far as directions are concerned, map coordinates can lead an individual to any location on the planet. 27 CLUB members seemingly migrated toward common coordinates for their final days. The numbers associated with longitude (East vs. West) and latitude (North vs. South) were first used centuries ago to designate geographic locations. A compass also uses numbers to specify more precise directions, such as "12 Degrees North."

Numbers are components of music, from half-notes, to line and stanza numbers, to concerto designations. Numbers are integral parts of our daily lives. It would be nearly impossible to navigate civilization in their absence.

N

W + E

S

FROM: "TWENTY SEVENDING" © 2013

"Could it be, they were all, riding on a storm?
Zodiac, looking back, causes for alarm?
Was the Cancer hiding, in Aquarius?
Libra? Leo? Virgo? Sagittarius?"

Humans attempt to form patterns in what would otherwise be a perpetual state of randomness. If someone was born into a family as the 7th child on the 7th day of the 7th month in 1977 at 7:07 AM, which also happened to be a Saturday (7th day of the week), there is an extremely noticeable pattern. Also, consider the possibility this person's first driver's license ended with a 7, and there was a 7 in the license plate number on this person's car, and the vehicle identification number had 77 as the first two digits. This constitutes a totally obvious pattern.

Numbers are also used to define categories. This person would have the zodiac sign of Cancer since July 7th falls between June 21st and July 22nd. Some may scoff at any correlation beyond a statistical probability, and some may remark at the coincidence, while others might insist there is an outside force influencing these repeating 7s. Did it just happen that way, or does it represent something purposefully woven into the fabric of our reality?

CANCER
JUNE 21 - JULY 22

FROM: "TWENTY SEVENDING" © 2013

"Things that would lead, to chaos and confusion
And fame and glory, became an intrusion
Rising star, shooting star, star turns into dust
Lost the will, broken still, taken from the lust"

Long ago, Greek Civilization grouped stars into patterns and thus named the constellations. We now know some of these "stars" are actually galaxies. Many are nowhere near the other stars that form the constellations as they were conceived only in the two perceived dimensions of height and width, while not accounting for depth. Meteors were categorized as "falling stars" in an attempt to explain streaks of disappearing light in the nighttime sky. That "theory" proved false. However, pattern designation continues into these modern times as a means to explain various phenomena, such as "things happen in threes," as well as scientifically proven patterns.

And what exactly is a star? A star can be simply described as a mass of incandescent gas. More detailed scientific definitions can consume several lines of text. A star can also be defined as an exceptionally talented performer with a large number of fans.

CELESTIAL PHENOMENA

THE BIG SIX

BRIAN JONES, "THE ROLLING STONES"

JIMI HENDRIX

JANIS JOPLIN

JIM MORRISON, "THE DOORS"

KURT COBAIN, "NIRVANA"

AMY WINEHOUSE

Dozens of musicians have died at the age of 27, but the most famous and their dates of death are:

"THE BIG SIX"
1. Brian Jones of the Rolling Stones (d. 07/03/1969)
2. Jimi Hendrix   (d. 09/18/1970)
3. Janis Joplin   (d. 10/04/1970)
4. Jim Morrison of The Doors   (d. 07/03/1971)
5. Kurt Cobain of Nirvana   (d. 04/05/1994)
6. Amy Winehouse   (d. 07/23/2011)

THE BIG 6

DEATH WITHIN FIRST FIVE DAYS OF A MONTH

BRIAN JONES   3RD

JIM MORRISON   3RD

JANIS JOPLIN   4TH

KURT COBAIN   5TH

3, 4, & 5 FORM THE BASIS FOR MUCH OF GEOMETRY AS

$$3^2 + 4^2 = 5^2; \text{ or } 9 + 16 = 25$$

shortest side = 3, longest side = 5, and the final side = 4

A TRIANGLE WITH THESE PROPORTIONS WILL HAVE A 90 DEGREE ANGLE AND WILL FIT THE DESCRIPTION OF A RIGHT TRIANGLE. THIS IS DERIVED FROM THE PYTHAGOREAN EQUATION.

"THE CORE FOUR" (Jones, Hendrix, Joplin, and Morrison) died over the exact period of 2 years, from 7/3/69 to 7/3/71! The total number of days between these 7/3 dates is 730. Not only did Jones and Morrison both die on July 3rd at the age of 27, but in 1969 AND 1971, July 3rd fell within the 27th calendar week of the year!

If the member with the latest calendar death week is removed (Joplin, during the 41st week), the average number of calendar weeks into the year of death for the remaining five is 27. Cobain at 15 weeks, Jones at 27 weeks, Morrison at 27 weeks, Winehouse at 30 weeks, and Hendrix falling within the 38th week.

(15 + 27 + 27 + 30 + 38 = 137, divided by 5 is 27.4, which rounds off to 27). Amy Winehouse died 30 calendar weeks into her year of death, doubling the 15 weeks calculated for the other non-CORE FOUR member, Kurt Cobain.

Note that four of the BIG SIX died within the first 5 days of their death months (3rd, 3rd, 4th, and 5th), as correlated with the Pythagorean Equation example.

In any given calendar year, the first death anniversary belongs to Kurt Cobain on 4/5, and the last death anniversary belongs to Janis Joplin on 10/4. Jones and Morrison fall directly in the middle on 7/3. This 6-month period contains all death anniversaries including Winehouse and Hendrix, and leaves a following 6-month period with no death anniversaries whatsoever. This forms another profound grouping pattern within the 27 CLUB.

APR 5--------------------OCT 4
THIS 6 MONTH PERIOD CONTAINS ALL DEATH ANNIVERSARIES

OCT 5--------------------APR 4
THIS 6 MONTH PERIOD CONTAINS NO DEATH ANNIVERSARIES

COBAIN COINCIDENCES

BIRTH DATE 02/20/1967: 0+2+2+0+1+9+6+7 = 27

BORN IN '67, 6 + 7 = 13

DIED IN '94, 9 + 4 = 13

DIED IN THE 4TH MONTH ON THE 5TH DAY, 6 YEARS PRIOR TO THE

     NEW MILLENNIUM (4,5,6 SEQUENCE)

DIED 16 DAYS FOLLOWING THE SPRING EQUINOX

DIED ON A DAY OF THE WEEK

     THAT FOLLOWS THE DAY BORN (MON - TUES)

BORN THE YEAR OF THE MONTEREY POP FESTIVAL ('67)

DIED IN SEATTLE WHERE HENDRIX WAS BORN

DIED AT 48 DEG N, AVERAGE BIG SIX DEATH LATITUDE

YEAR DIED = HENDRIX'S BIRTH YEAR + DEATH LATITUDE

     '94 = '42 + 52

WIFE (COURTNEY LOVE) LOST COBAIN, (DIED AGE 27)

     LOST BAND MATE, KRISTEN PFAFF, (DIED AGE 27)

     LOST BAND MATE, PETE DeFREITAS, (DIED AGE 27)

After the last of the CORE FOUR (Morrison) passed away in 1971, it was 23 years later that Kurt Cobain died in 1994. When Amy Winehouse followed, it was on the 23rd of July, 2011, a repeat of the number 23. Additionally, the average number of letters in each of the BIG SIX's names is 11 as was the year of Amy Winehouse's death. If the digits in Winehouse's year of birth are added (8+3), the answer is 11, which was the year of her death, 2011. Oddly enough, if the year Winehouse was born ('83) is added to the year Winehouse died ('11), the answer is '94 which is the year her 27 CLUB predecessor, Cobain, died. There are 11 months between Jones' birth and Joplin's birth... the only two whose last names begin with a "J." When Jimi Hendrix was born on 11/27/42, it was almost 9 months to the day after Brian Jones was born on 2/28/42. This means that Jimi Hendrix could have been conceived on the day Brian Jones was born!

Numerology is any belief in the divine or mystical relationship between a number and coinciding events. Could there be a gray zone between Mathematics and Numerology?

MATH...
NUMEROLOGY

"J" COINCIDENCES

"J"ANIS "J"OPLIN – BORN IN "J"ANUARY

"J"ONES, BRIAN

"J"IMI HENDRIX

"J"IM MORRISON

"J"ADE – AMY WINEHOUSE'S MIDDLE NAME

"J"ANIS IS AMY WINEHOUSE'S MOTHER'S NAME

"J" IMMEDIATLEY PRECEDES "K" IN THE ALPHABET – "K"URT COBAIN

"J"ULY 3RD - MARKS BEGINNING AND END OF CORE FOUR DEATHS

"J"ULY – JONES, MORRISON, AND WINEHOUSE ALL DIED THIS MONTH

"J"ULY – DEATH MONTH FOR CORE FOUR WHO DID NOT PERFORM AT
WOODSTOCK – BRIAN "J"ONES AND "J"IM MORRISON

"J"UNE 1967 – "J"IMI & "J"ANIS PLAYED @ MONTEREY POP FESTIVAL

"J"AMES – THE LEGAL NAME FOR BOTH "J"IMI AND "J"IM

"J"OHNNY – "J"IMI'S FIRST NAME AT BIRTH

"J"UNE 27TH – IN 2008, WINEHOUSE SANG FOR MANDELA'S
90TH BIRTHDAY

"J"ULY 27TH – ROGER LEE DURHAM (BLOODSTONE) DIED AT AGE 27

When the 27 CLUB became a phenomenon, the next most recognized pattern was the recurring "J" as a first letter in the names of the CORE FOUR. Notably, "J"anis "J"oplin has both first and last names beginning with a "J." There are also "J"ones, "J"imi, and "J"im. It appears Kurt Cobain broke the pattern of the CORE FOUR. However, "K" immediately follows "J" in the alphabet. The position of "K" immediately following "J" in the alphabet provides a permanent welding of these letters and Cobain's connected proximity. Amy Winehouse's middle name is…"J"ade. Amy Winehouse's mother's name is, "J"anis, spelled exactly the same way as "J"anis Joplin. And Janis Winehouse was 27 years old when she gave birth to Amy!

J,K

JOPLIN COINCIDENCES

JOPLIN'S DEATH LATITUDE DIVIDED BY JONES' DEATH LATITUDE IS

34/51, OR 0.66666666 ....

HALFWAY BETWEEN JOPLIN'S AND MORRISON'S DEATH LATITUDES IS

WOODSTOCK, NY, AT 41.5 DEGREES N.

JOPLIN'S DAY + MONTH (BIRTH) = COBAIN'S DAY (BIRTH)

19 + 1 = 20

DIED IN A CITY BEGINNING WITH "LO" ("LO"S ANGELES) LIKE HENDRIX

AND WINEHOUSE ("LO"NDON)

BORN IN A MONTH THAT BEGINS WITH "J" (JANUARY), AND

FIRST AND LAST NAMES BEGIN WITH "J."

SHARED 1970 AS HER DEATH YEAR WITH HENDRIX

SHARED THE STAGE AT BOTH MONTEREY POP FESTIVAL AND

WOODSTOCK WITH HENDRIX

DIED WITHIN 2 DEGREES OF THE 120TH WEST MERIDIAN LIKE COBAIN

JANIS PASSED AWAY 27 DAYS BEFORE HALLOWEEN

Janis Joplin (with two "J"s) was the only member to be born during a month that begins with "J" (January). Another calendar location the "J" surfaces for the CORE FOUR is the month of "J"uly, when the two-year span of time began and ended with the deaths of all CORE FOUR members. Amazingly, the CORE FOUR artists who have "J"uly dates of death (Jones and Morrison) had NOT performed at Woodstock which took place in 1969 (Jones was already deceased). Both Jimi and Janis DID perform at Woodstock and died within a little over one year from those performances. Jimi Hendrix died exactly 13 months to the day after Woodstock. Jimi and Janis would also be the only two to die within the same calendar year (1970). Cobain was only 2 years old when Woodstock took place (Kurt Cobain's mother would eventually add "Club" to the 27 phenomenon when she was interviewed shortly after his death, although this is still debated). Winehouse would not be born for another 14 years after Woodstock but would eventually die during "J"uly of 2011.

Does this make a case for Alphabetology?

ALPHABETOLOGY

13s

13th – DAY OF SUMMER JONES/MORRISON DIE

13 – FULL MOONS, JONES'/MORRISON'S DEATH YEARS

13 – FULL MOONS, JONES'/HENDRIX'S BIRTH YEAR

13 – MONTHS FROM WOODSTOCK TO HENDRIX'S DEATH

13 – DAYS NEEDED TO SURPASS 10,000 IN JONES' LIFE

13 – WEEKS BETWEEN COBAIN'S & JONES'/MORRISON'S

     DEATH ANNIVERSARIES

13 – WEEKS BETWEEN JONES'/MORRISON'S AND

     JOPLIN'S DEATH ANNIVERSARY

13 – WEEKS BETWEEN SOLSTICES AND EQUINOXES

13 - MONTHS BETWEEN HENDRIX'S/MORRISON'S BIRTHS

13 – YEARS AFTER JOPLIN'S DEATH, WINEHOUSE IS BORN

13 – SUM OF COBAIN'S DEATH YEAR DIGITS, 9 + 4

13 – SUM OF COBAIN'S BIRTH YEAR DIGITS, 6 + 7

NUMBER OF DAYS AMY WINEHOUSE WAS 27 IS 313

Morrison and Jones died on the 13th day of Summer during the 27th calendar week of their death years ('69 and '71). Although most years can only account for 12 full moons, Brian Jones and Jim Morrison died in years that had 13 full moons. Winehouse was born 13 years after Joplin and Hendrix died. Hendrix's and Morrison's births span 13 months. If the 3rd day of July which contains the Jones/Morrison deaths is used as a reference point, 13 weeks prior marks the death anniversary of Kurt Cobain and 13 weeks after marks the death anniversary of Janis Joplin. There are 13 weeks in each season of the year. There are subsequently also 13 weeks between equinoxes and solstices that demarcate the seasons.

Brian Jones would live for 9,988 days; it would have taken 13 more days to surpass the mark of 10,000. Amy Winehouse would be 27 years old for 313 days. The total of all BIG SIX birthday digits is 113, also ending in 13. There is only a 1 in 100 chance that either of these numbers would end in 13. It is even more unlikely that both numbers would end in 13.

Add the digits in Cobain's birth year (6+7) and it equals 13. Add the digits in Cobain's death year (9+4) and it also equals 13. From the dates of Woodstock (8/15 to 8/18/69) until Joplin's death is 13.5 months, which is half of 27. Hendrix died 13 months TO THE DAY after Woodstock on 9/18/70.

13

DEATH DEMOGRAPHIC PATTERNS

NATIONALITY	GENDER
BRITISH	MALE
AMERICAN	MALE
AMERICAN	FEMALE
AMERICAN	MALE
AMERICAN	MALE
BRITISH	FEMALE

BIG SIX DEATHS BEGIN AND END WITH THE BRITISH

FEMALES DIED 40 YEARS APART, AND AT NORTHERN AND SOUTHERN BIG SIX EXTREMES OF LATITUDE, LONDON & LOS ANGELES. BOTH CITIES BEGIN WITH "LO", AND ARE NEAR THE WESTERN COASTS OF THEIR RESPECTIVE CONTINENTS

Since Jones died in 1969 and Winehouse died in 2011, the timespan between the beginning and end of BIG SIX deaths is 42 years, and Jones was born in '42. This span is situated across 6 decades, but only barely. Jones died in 1969, the last year of the '60s; Winehouse died in 2011, the second year of the '10s. With the 42-year span of deaths positioned in this manner, it is as though the British members, Jones and Winehouse, provide the "bookends" of the BIG SIX.

The remaining MIDDLE FOUR were all Americans (Hendrix, Joplin, Morrison, and Cobain). The pattern of death (as well as birth) for the BIG SIX is male, male, female, male, male, female. Cobain died on 4/5, 6 years before Y2K (the year 2000 and the transition to a new millennium). The first five of the BIG SIX died during the prior millennium (the year 1000 through the year 1999). Winehouse was the only one of the BIG SIX to die during the current millennium (2000 through 2999).

Y2K

MILITARY CONFLICTS

JONES, HENDRIX, JOPLIN, AND MORRISON WERE BORN DURING WWII AND DIED DURING THE VIETNAM WAR

COBAIN WAS BORN DURING THE VIETNAM WAR AND DIED DURING THE CIVIL WAR IN BOSNIA

WINEHOUSE WAS BORN DURING CONFLICTS IN GRENADA AND LEBANON, AND DIED DURING THE WAR IN AFGHANISTAN

The CORE FOUR, with dates of death ranging from 7/3/69 to 7/3/71, all fall within the timeframe of U.S. troop involvement in the Vietnam War. Jimi Hendrix actually served as a member of the 101st Airborne Division for a brief period. Hendrix and Joplin were born only 54 days apart which is two 27-day periods. They died 16 days apart. They could have traded their dates of death and died OUT of birth order, and still have been 27. However, the CORE FOUR all died during that precise 2-year period from 7/3/69 to 7/3/71 in the same order as their births.

WAR

BIRTH DATES OF THE BIG SIX

1. BRIAN JONES	02/28/42
2. JIMI HENDRIX	11/27/42
3. JANIS JOPLIN	01/19/43
4. JIM MORRISON	12/08/43
5. KURT COBAIN	02/20/67
6. AMY WINEHOUSE	09/14/83

The CORE FOUR were all born in 1942 and 1943 during World War II. Jimi Hendrix's father actually served during WWII. Notably, both BIG SIX members whose LAST names begin with "J", (Jones and Joplin) were born during the FIRST two months of their birth years. Beyond the CORE FOUR, Kurt Cobain was also born during the FIRST two months of his birth year, totaling 3 of the BIG SIX within that pattern. Equally notable is that both "Jims" (Jimi Hendrix and Jim Morrison, whose FIRST names begin with "J") were born during the LAST two months of their birth years. This means that 5 of the BIG SIX members were born in the first 2 or the last 2 months of the year. While Jimi Hendrix and Jim Morrison were born during Fall, Jones, Joplin, and Cobain were born during Winter. Only Amy Winehouse was born outside of the first 2 or last 2 months of her birth year on September 14th, approaching the end of Summer. There were no Spring births.

Winehouse has the same number of letters in her birth month (September) as does her last name (9 in each); Morrison (December) has 8 in each, and he was born on the 8th! Additionally, all BIG SIX members died during the second half of their years of death except for the one who has no "J" in his name at all....Kurt Cobain died in April.

CORE FOUR BORN DURING WWII

PARTIAL NAMESAKES

<u>FATHER</u>	<u>SON</u>
LEWIS BLOUNT JONES	LEWIS BRIAN HOPKINS JONES
JAMES ALLEN HENDRIX	JAMES MARSHALL HENDRIX
DONALD LELAND COBAIN	KURT DONALD COBAIN

Three of the four males are named in part after their fathers, though there was no bona fide "Junior" in the group. Lewis Brian Hopkins Jones was named after his father, Lewis Blount Jones. James Marshall "Jimi" Hendrix was named after his father, James Allen Hendrix, and his late uncle, Leon Marshall Hendrix. Hendrix was actually originally named Johnny Allen Hendrix, but his parents changed his name when he was a toddler. Kurt Donald Cobain was named after his father, Donald Leland Cobain. George Stephen Morrison (who eventually became an Admiral in the U.S. Navy and served during the Vietnam War) was the father of James Douglas Morrison, the only male within the BIG SIX who did not receive his father's first or middle name.

FATHER

AGE AT PARENTS' DIVORCE

HENDRIX	9
COBAIN	9
WINEHOUSE	+ 9
COMBINED AGES	27

Half of the BIG SIX experienced the divorce of their parents during childhood. Jimi Hendrix, Kurt Cobain, and Amy Winehouse would all eventually divulge how this influenced many aspects of their music. Perhaps the most affected was Cobain whose mother was reported to have "run off" with a longshoreman. Multiple sources reference his parents' divorce as a major contributor to Cobain's "defiance of authority."

Divorce was less common in their time, so the 50% rate among the BIG SIX was somewhat remarkable. That each of these three superstars was 9 years old at the time of their parent's divorce is a long shot. But to also consider the sum of their ages would total 27 is markedly difficult to believe, even if they had fit a more random pattern such as 6, 8, and 13 which would also total 27. The odds for each of them to have been 9 years old during those trying times are simply astonishing.

9, 9, 9

BIRTHDAY SUMS

STAR	BIRTHDAY	SUM
HENDRIX	11/27/42	1+1+2+7+4+2=17
COBAIN	2/20/67	2+2+0+6+7=17
JONES	2/28/42	2+2+8+4+2=18
JOPLIN	1/19/43	1+1+9+4+3=18
MORRISON	12/8/43	1+2+8+4+3=18
WINEHOUSE	9/14/83	9+1+4+8+3=25

THE SUM TOTAL OF 17+17+18+18+18+25 = 1<u>13</u>

ANOTHER APPEARANCE OF THE NUMBER 13!

Patterns can be found when comparing sequences within sets of numbers. When searching patterns of birthdates expressed as MM/DD/YY, there is a simple process of taking each digit within the sequence and adding them together. For example, the very first U.S. Veteran's Day of this millennium occurred on November 11, 2000. Expressed as MM/DD/YY, the sequence becomes 11/11/00. If all digits in the sequence are added as 1+1+1+1+0+0, the total is 4. Another example for purposes of illustration could be the last Leap Day of the prior millennium. 02/29/96, when added as 0+2+2+9+9+6 equals 28.

LEAP DAY

WINEHOUSE COINCIDENCES

52 = NUMBER OF DAYS MISSED FROM A FULL 27TH YEAR

52 = DEATH LATITUDE

DEATH DAY = MONTH + DAY OF BIRTH

$$23 = 9 + 14$$

23RD LETTER OF THE ALPHABET IS "W"

23 YEARS BETWEEN MORRISON'S AND COBAIN'S DEATHS

BIRTH YEAR PLUS DEATH YEAR = COBAIN'S DEATH YEAR;

$$'83 + '11 = '94$$

ONLY BIG SIX MEMBER TO BE BORN AND DIE IN THE

SAME CITY (LONDON)

DEATH YEAR = SUM OF BIRTH YEAR DIGITS;

$$'11 = 8 + 3$$

BORN WITH ALL OTHER BIG SIX MEMBERS IN THE LAST

MILLENNIUM, BUT THE ONLY MEMBER WHO DIED

DURING THE CURRENT MILLENNIUM

Amy Winehouse is the only member to fall beyond the birth pattern of being born within the first two or last two months of the year. She was born and died in the second half of each respective year. She also breaks another date of birth pattern: If each digit in the birth dates of the other BIG SIX members is added, the sum is either 17 or 18. But, Amy Winehouse's totals 25. She was also the only BIG SIX member to experience birth during the prior millennium and death in the current millennium.

1983 – 2011
AMY WINEHOUSE WAS BORN AND DIED DURING DIFFERENT MILLENNIA

FROM: "TWENTY SEVENDING" © 2013

"Was it the Vietnam protest, in our streets?
Was it the Bay of Pigs, and a naval fleet?
Upon the line of the Tropic of Cancer?
Should we look to the stars to find the answer?"

Dates of birth and death produce more numerical coincidences. If the day of the month and the year Jones was born are added together (28 + '42), the answer is the year Hendrix, died ('70). If the day of the month and year Hendrix was born are added (27 + '42), the answer is the year Jones died ('69). In other words, month plus year Jones was born is the year Hendrix died and vice versa!

If Winehouse's birth month and birth day are added (9 + 14), the answer is 23 (her death day).

If Hendrix's death month and death day are added (9 + 18), the answer is 27 (his birth day).

If the days of the month upon which Joplin and Morrison were born are added together (19 + 8), the answer is 27.

Birthday sums previously addressed yield totals of 17, 18, or 25 for the BIG SIX. These were totals of the digits as MM/DD/YY. An astounding total for two BIG SIX members arises when using four digits for the birth year as MM/DD/YYYY. Jimi Hendrix's equation becomes 1+1+2+7+1+9+4+2 = 27! Kurt Cobain's equation is 0+2+2+0+1+9+6+7 which also equals 27!

27

FROM: "TWENTY SEVENDING" © 2013

"Come as you are, because no two are the same
Say no to rehab, makes love a losing game
Spring becomes Summer, Summer turns into Fall
How does early Winter make sense of it all?"

There are additional birth date curiosities.

Kurt Cobain was born on the 20th of his birth month.

If Joplin's birth month and birth day are added (1 + 19), the answer is 20. If Morrison's birth month and birth day are added (12 + 8) the answer is 20.

Joplin was born on the 19th and Cobain follows immediately on the 20th of his birth month.

Hendrix was born on the 27th and Jones follows immediately on the 28th of his birth month.

BIRTH DATE CURIOSITIES

BIRTH ZODIAC PATTERNS

CAPRICORN	PISCES	VIRGO	SAGITTARIUS
JOPLIN	JONES	WINEHOUSE	HENDRIX
	COBAIN		MORRISON

Every birth date falls under a sign of the zodiac:

Brian Jones: February 28th
                Pisces (February 19th to March 20th)

Jimi Hendrix: November 27th
                Sagittarius (November 22nd to December 21st)

Janis Joplin: January 19th
                Capricorn (December 22nd to January 20th)

Jim Morrison: December 8th
                Sagittarius (November 22nd to December 21st)

Kurt Cobain: February 20th
                Pisces (February 19th to March 20th)

Amy Winehouse: September 14th
                Virgo (August 23rd to September 22nd)

The pattern that emerges shows 1 female and 2 males being born during the first half of the year, and 1 female and 2 males being born in the second half of the year. Additionally, each female has a Zodiac Sign uniquely her own and each male shares a Zodiac Sign with one other male.

ZODIAC

DEATH ZODIAC PATTERNS

ARIES	**CANCER**	**VIRGO**	**LIBRA**
COBAIN	JONES	HENDRIX	JOPLIN
	MORRISON		
	WINEHOUSE		

THE SIGN OF CANCER CLAIMED THE FIRST AND LAST, WHETHER REFERENCING THE BIG SIX, OR THE CORE FOUR. THE ANCIENT SYMBOL FOR CANCER RESEMBLES THE NUMBER 69 ('69 IS JONES' YEAR OF DEATH AND THE YEAR OF WOODSTOCK).

Interestingly, 3 of the BIG SIX would die under the influence of the Zodiac sign of Cancer (Jones, Morrison, and Winehouse who was in the Cancer-Leo cusp, although some astrological sources argue that July 23rd is under the sign of Cancer only). Since Cancer begins "J"une 21st and extends through "J"uly 22nd, it is the only Zodiac sign to begin and end during months that begin with the "J" that provides a link to so many 27 CLUB commonalities. The ancient symbol for the Zodiac sign of Cancer resembles the number "69," the year of Jones' death and the year of Woodstock. The first and last of the CORE FOUR (Jones and Morrison) died under the sign of Cancer, as well as the first and last of the BIG SIX (Jones and Winehouse). Strikingly, the 27 CLUB formed under the sign of Cancer, and both the CORE FOUR and the BIG SIX were completed under the sign of Cancer.

69

DAY OF THE WEEK BORN/DIED

	SUN	MON	TUE	WED	THU	FRI	SAT
BORN	X	KC	JJ	JM		JH	BJ
				AW			
DIED	X	JJ	KC		BJ	JH	JM
							AW

Days of the week regarding birth and death reveal a series of patterns.

	BORN ON	**DIED ON**
Brian Jones	Saturday	Thursday
Jimi Hendrix	Friday	Friday
Janis Joplin	Tuesday	Monday
Jim Morrison	Wednesday	Saturday
Kurt Cobain	Monday	Tuesday
Amy Winehouse	Wednesday	Saturday

S M T W T F S

FROM: "TWENTY SEVENDING" © 2013

"Your passions paid off, from the early stages
Could sing a book, in a couple of pages
Fame that came forth, from Morpheus in a dream
On top of the world, better than it could seem"

Sunday remains untouched for all days of birth and death. Additionally, no one died on Wednesday, and no one was born on Thursday. Jim Morrison and Amy Winehouse, who are designated last of the CORE FOUR and BIG SIX, share Wednesday as their days of birth and Saturday as their days of death. Hendrix was the only member to be born and die on the same day of the week, which was Friday. Joplin was born on a Tuesday and died on a Monday. Just the opposite, Cobain was born on a Monday and died on a Tuesday. He was the only member to die on a day of the week immediately following a day of birth. Jones was the only member associated with a Thursday, and it marked his day of death.

CALENDAR PATTERNS

PLACES OF BIRTH

STAR	PLACE OF BIRTH	DEATH
WINEHOUSE	LONDON	LONDON
HENDRIX	SEATTLE, WA	LONDON
COBAIN	ABERDEEN, WA	SEATTLE, WA
JONES	GLOUCESTERSHIRE	E. SUSSEX
MORRISON	MELBOURNE, FL	PARIS
JOPLIN	PORT ARTHUR, TX	LOS ANGELES

There are stark contrasts regarding birthplace, location of death, and distance between these cities for the BIG SIX:

	Birthplace	Location of Death	Distance
Brian Jones	Gloucestershire, England	E. Sussex, England	179 mi.
Jimi Hendrix	Seattle, WA, USA	London, England	4781 mi.
Janis Joplin	Port Arthur, TX, USA	Los Angeles, CA, USA	1639 mi.
Jim Morrison	Melbourne, FL, USA	Paris, France	4475 mi.
Kurt Cobain	Aberdeen, WA, USA	Seattle, WA, USA	109 mi.
Amy Winehouse	London, England	London, England	0 mi.

However, within these contrasting sets of distances are yet more patterns.

DISTANCES

FROM: "TWENTY SEVENDING" © 2013

"We saw such perfection through the telescope
You criticized yourself, beneath a microscope
Can't see you in daylight, only in the dark
Ringing like a riddle, leaving such a mark"

Notably, Winehouse is the only one of the BIG SIX to experience birth and death in the same city (London). Furthermore, Winehouse and Jones were both born in England. Hendrix also died in London, making London the only city to lay a final claim to two of the BIG SIX. Three members (Hendrix, Winehouse, and Joplin) died in a city beginning with the letters "Lo" (two in "Lo"ndon, plus one in "Lo"s Angeles). Cobain and Hendrix were both born in the State of Washington. Cobain died in Seattle, where Hendrix was born. Jones and Joplin died in the same countries where they were born. Additionally, both "Jims" outdistanced the separation of birthplace and location of death by more than double that of the other 4 combined (over 4,000 miles each) and died in countries foreign to their births.

LO..., LO..., LO...

FROM: "TWENTY SEVENDING" © 2013

"Not even 400 moons, that shone so bright
Just like a meteor...the rock turns to light
So beautiful and brief, the thrill turns to grief
Beyond a celestial barrier reef"

The remaining Jones, plus Joplin, plus Cobain, plus Winehouse only total 1,927 miles of birth and death location separation. Jones and Cobain show relatively short distances (179 and 109, respectively). The difference between these distances (179 – 109) is '70, which is the year both Hendrix and Joplin died. Interestingly, an automotive round trip for Morrison (Melbourne, Florida) or Joplin (Port Arthur, Texas) to visit the other's hometown today would take 27 hours.

A most remarkable coincidence involves the average of all distances between birthplace and location of death for the BIG SIX: If the average distance (1864) is divided by Brian Jones' year of death ('69), the answer is 27!

MELBOURNE TO PORT ARTHUR ROUND TRIP 27 HOURS

"H" DEATH SETTING

HOME – JONES, MORRISON, COBAIN, WINEHOUSE

HOTEL – HENDRIX, JOPLIN

OTHER 27'S DEATH SETTINGS

HOME – RON "PIGPEN" McKERNAN

HOME – KRISTEN PFAFF, HOLE

HEADING HOME ON FOOT – MIA ZAPATA, GITS

HOSPITAL – DAVE ALEXANDER, STOOGES

HORSE – ROGER DURHAM, BLOODSTONE

HILLSIDE – AL WILSON, CANNED HEAT

HIGHWAY – PETE de FREITAS, ECHO AND...BUNNYMEN

While "J" establishes a pattern with BIG SIX names, followed by the bridging "K" of Kurt Cobain, and the "L" which is strongly represented in cities of death, "H" is affiliated with the settings of their deaths. Each of the BIG SIX died at "H"ome or in a "H"otel. In fact, 4 died at "H"ome and 2 died in a "H"otel. Of the two 27 CLUB members that London claimed, one was in a "H"otel (Hendrix) and the other was at "H"ome (Winehouse).

Jones died at "H"ome (Cotchford Farm, the setting inspiration for Winnie the Pooh). Hendrix died in a "H"otel (London). Joplin died in a "H"otel (Los Angeles). Morrison died at "H"ome (Paris). Cobain died at "H"ome (Seattle). Last of the BIG SIX, Winehouse died at "H"ome in London. The two "H"otel deaths of Hendrix and Joplin occurred in 1970, the only double death year for the BIG SIX.

Interestingly, Morrison and his girlfriend had reportedly made their home in Paris for many reasons in spite of Jim being a citizen of the United States. The deciding moment stemmed from the advice of Jim's lawyer as Jim was facing possible jail time following an arrest in the United States. At the time, the United States and France did not have an extradition treaty that would apply to Jim's charges. When Jim first arrived in Paris, he checked into a "H"otel and lived there for approximately two months before settling into his new "H"ome with his girlfriend.

HOME
HOTEL

FROM: "TWENTY SEVENDING" © 2013

"Only stayed around, for two dozen and three
Still so very young; couldn't wait to be free?
Love of your fans, it was platinum and gold
Beautiful Borealis, but seems so cold!"

Both "H"ome and "H"otel begin with an "H." Some other 27s who died at "H"ome were Ron "Pigpen" McKernan of the "Grateful Dead," Pete Ham of "Badfinger," and Kristen Pfaff of "Hole." There are alternative places that begin with "H" where musical celebrities have died. Some made it to a "H"ospital before they died. Dave Alexander, percussionist for "The Stooges," was admitted to the "H"ospital in 1975 for pancreatitis associated with his heavy drinking. He developed pulmonary edema as a complication of his disease and died at the age of 27. Pete de Freitas, 27, of "Echo and the Bunnymen" died in a motorcycle crash on a "H"ighway in Europe. 27-year-old Al Wilson of "Canned Heat" was found dead on a "H"illside in Topanga, California. His death was labeled as an accidental acute barbiturate intoxication. Roger Lee Durham, singer and percussionist with "Bloodstone," died in 1973 on July 27th, at the age of 27 from injuries sustained when he fell off a "H"orse.

HOSPITAL
HORSE
HIGHWAY

FROM: TWENTY SEVENDING © 2013

"The Sun set too soon, since your dusk never came
Way too much was lost, we want something to blame
Equinox, paradox, what were the reasons?
Hard knocks sealed the locks, hundred and eight
seasons"

"H"elicopters have also proven fatal to music celebrities. Stevie Ray Vaughan, 35, founder of "Blues Rock" died with the pilot and three members of Eric Clapton's crew in a "H"elicopter crash and though none of these stars were 27 years old, it occurred in 1990 on August 27th.

For further comparison, a rather famous "A"irplane accident involving other musicians who were not 27 years old led to "..the day the music died" (referencing 2/3/1959) as proclaimed by Don McLean in his 1971 release "American Pie." It hit number 1 the following year. 28-year-old Perry Richardson, Jr. (a.k.a Big Bopper, known for "Chantilly Lace") and 17-year-old Ritchie Valens ("La Bamba") were killed. Of most fame on the plane with Richardson and Valens that day, was Buddy Holly who died at the age of 22, very well known for "That'll Be The Day"... ("when I die.")

However, with numerous possibilities and alternatives for other words beginning with "H," and 25 other letters of the alphabet to label death settings, the BIG SIX were all limited to "H"ome or "H"otel as the pattern for their places of death.

NO HELICOPTERS
NO AIRPLANES
FOR BIG SIX DEATHS

NORTH – SOUTH DEATH PATTERN

STAR	DEATH LATITUDE
WINEHOUSE	52 DEGREES NORTH
HENDRIX	52 DEGREES NORTH
JONES	51 DEGREES NORTH
MORRISON	49 DEGREES NORTH
COBAIN	48 DEGREES NORTH
JOPLIN	34 DEGREES NORTH

There are significant numbers associated with birthplaces and locations of death. Every location on this planet is associated with a specific longitude and latitude. While latitude designates how far North or South a particular place is located, longitude designates an East vs. West position. If the Earth is compared to an orange, longitude may be explained as looking down onto the top of the orange and making pie-shaped slices all the way through the bottom. This results in "orange wedges." Again, looking down from the top of the Earth and not thinking about the actual spherical nature of the planet, one visualizes more of a circle which is divided into 360 degrees.

As there are 24 hours in a day, there are 24 imaginary longitudinal lines on the globe, 15 degrees apart. These meridians (longitudinal lines) are the guidelines for our time zones. Meridians can be even more specific by referencing a single degree, or even smaller measurements. The Prime Meridian runs through Greenwich, England, and has been designated 0 degrees longitude, from which all other longitudes are referenced. When the 360 degrees of longitude that span the planet are grouped into East and West halves, there is never a number greater than 180. For instance, 120 degrees East is very close to Shanghai, China, while 120 degrees West is very near Los Angeles, California. Longitudinal lines are approximately the same length when measuring continuously around the globe.

LATITUDE
LONGITUDE

MORRISON COINCIDENCES

8 - # OF LETTERS IN LAST NAME

8 - # OF LETTERS IN BIRTH MONTH

8 - DAY OF MONTH BORN

DIED EXACTLY 2 YEARS TO THE DAY AFTER JONES

DIED DURING THE 27TH CALENDAR WEEK OF 1971

DIED ON THE 13TH DAY OF SUMMER

BORN ON A WEDNESDAY AND DIED ON A SATURDAY LIKE
WINEHOUSE

10,070 - # TOTAL DAYS LIVED AND IS THE EXACT AVERAGE
TOTAL DAYS FOR BIG SIX.

208 - # OF DAYS BEING 27 AND BIG SIX AVERAGE IS 208

DAY + MONTH (BIRTH) = COBAIN'S DAY OF BIRTH

8 + 12 = 20

SHARES BIRTHDAY DIGIT SUM OF 18 WITH JOPLIN/JONES

GIRLFRIEND, PAMELA COURSON, DIED AT AGE 27

Lines of latitude, however, are somewhat different from longitude in that none of the Northern Latitudes are of equal length as they circle the globe, nor are any of the Southern Latitudes. Once again, using the orange as a model, if one is looking at an orange from the side, slices are taken horizontally, so a "slice" of equal thickness from side to side (instead of a wedge) is produced. Latitudinal lines are sometimes called "Parallels" as they never touch another line of latitude.

A slice taken at the Equator has a circumference of 24,901 miles. A slice taken at the Arctic Circle is only 10,975 miles in circumference. In comparison with half of the globe being 180 degrees for longitudes, the North and South designations for latitudes are divided into 90 degree halves, such that looking at the planet from the side, one would see the Equator in the middle at 0 degrees, and 90 degrees North would be the North Pole, while 90 degrees South would be the South Pole. New York City is 41 degrees North and New Orleans is 30 degrees North. However, Sao Paulo, Brazil is 23.5 degrees South as it is South of the equator. In general, latitudes are generally thought of in terms of every ten degrees but can also be referenced to a single degree or smaller. Compasses, maps, and Global Positioning System (GPS) devices use North-South and East-West orientation to aid with locations and direction of travel.

A single degree of latitude equals 69 miles (year of Jones death, again). Jim Morrison wrote the song, "Horse Latitudes!"

HORSE LATITUDES

LATITUDES AND CITIES OF DEATH

Amy Winehouse	52 degrees North (London)
Jimi Hendrix	52 degrees North (London)
Brian Jones	51 degrees North (East Sussex)
Jim Morrison	49 degrees North (Paris)
Kurt Cobain	48 degrees North (Seattle)
Janis Joplin	34 degrees North (Los Angeles)

The latitudes of death total 286. Coincidentally, the ground distance from London (death place of Hendrix and Winehouse) to Paris (death place of Morrison) is 287 miles. The average latitude of death, (286 divided by 6) is 48, the latitude where Cobain died. There is a "MIDDLE FOUR" lifespan calculation to be made for the Americans (Hendrix, Joplin, Morrison, and Cobain). Hendrix was born in '42, and Cobain died in '94. The difference between Hendrix's birth and Cobain's death is 52 years ('94 – '42 = 52), and 52 degrees North is where Hendrix and Winehouse died. There are 179 other possibilities for latitudes of death and two of the BIG SIX died at the very same latitude of 52 degrees North.

DEATH LATITUDES

FROM: "TWENTY SEVENDING" © 2013

"A drag getting old, three had ended their cruise
TWENTY SEVenDING had already made news
Exactly two years, from when the first one fell
The fourth one died, music cried, tolling of the bell"

Winehouse and Hendrix both died at 52 degrees North in London. Jones died at 51 degrees North in E. Sussex, England. Just beneath that latitude was Morrison at 49 degrees North in Paris. Just below that was Kurt Cobain at 48 degrees North in Seattle, Washington. Jones, Morrison, and Cobain died within 3 degrees separation of latitude. FAR beneath Cobain was Joplin at 34 degrees North in Los Angeles, California. In fact, both women died at the North-South extremes of latitude (52 and 34 degrees North). Five of the BIG SIX (Joplin omitted here) died within 4 degrees separation of latitude (48 North to 52 North). Amazingly, Woodstock was held in the State of New York at 41.5 degrees North which is precisely halfway between the death latitudes of Morrison and Joplin (49 North and 34 North). They were the last 2 of the CORE FOUR to die and the 2 who were born at the lowest latitudes (30 North and 28 North, respectively).

WOODSTOCK

BIRTH LATITUDE PATTERN

STAR	CITY	LATITUDE
JONES	GLOUCESTERSHIRE	52N
WINEHOUSE	LONDON	52N
HENDRIX	SEATTLE	48N
COBAIN	ABERDEEN	47N
JOPLIN	PORT ARTHUR	30N
MORRISON	MELBOURNE	28N

(0 DEGREE, 1 DEGREE OR 2 DEGREES SEPARATION)

The latitudes of birth demonstrate additional recognizable patterns. Jones and Winehouse were both born at 52 degrees North in Gloucestershire, England, and London, England. There was no separation of birth latitude. Hendrix's and Cobain's birthplaces were Seattle, WA (48 degrees North), and Aberdeen, WA (47 degrees North), so their birthplaces are separated by one degree of latitude. Joplin's and Morrison's birthplaces were Port Arthur, TX (30 degrees North) and Melbourne, FL (28 degrees North), so their birthplaces were separated by 2 degrees of latitude. So, in pairs, the BIG SIX's birthplaces were separated by either 0, 1, or 2 degrees of latitude! It is as though the southernmost birth latitude being Jim Morrison at 28 degrees North established the numerical bar of 28 as the age none of the BIX SIX would ever achieve.

BIRTH LATITUDE

CITIES OF DEATH SPELL "PARALLELS"

CITY OF DEATH	STAR
PARIS	MORRISON
LOS ANGELES	JOPLIN
LONDON	HENDRIX
EAST SUSSEX	JONES
LONDON	WINEHOUSE
SEATTLE	COBAIN

PAR AL L E L S

If the "Par" is taken from Paris for Morrison, and "LA" from Los Angeles for Joplin, and one "L" each from London for Hendrix and Winehouse, and the "E" from East Sussex for Jones, and the "S" from Seattle for Cobain, the word "PARALLELS" (another word for Latitudes) is formed from the BIG SIX's cities of death! Is this merely a coincidence?

Some people view an afterlife as a transition to a parallel universe. Without venturing into quotes of Einstein and Theory of Quantum Mechanics, a comprehensive look into the afterlife seems to beg the following question: If death is somehow linked to the concept of a Parallel Universe (or Parallel Universes), could the coincidences involving BIG SIX Longitudes and Latitudes be a reference to an association with either?

PARALLELS

DEATH LONGITUDES

STAR	DEATH LONGITUDE
WINEHOUSE	0 DEGREES/LONDON
HENDRIX	0 DEGREES/LONDON
JONES	0 DEGREES/SUSSEX
MORRISON	2 DEGREES E./PARIS
JOPLIN	118 DEGREES W./LA
COBAIN	122 DEGREES W./SEATTLE

(0 DEGREES IS CONSIDERED TO BE THE PRIME MERIDIAN...THE STARTING POINT FOR ALL LONGITUDINAL MEASUREMENTS)

Strikingly, 3 members (Jones, Hendrix, and Winehouse) died at 0 degrees longitude with 359 other longitudes as possibilities. Adding Morrison (2 degrees East) to this grouping, four members of the BIG SIX died within 2 degrees of the Prime Meridian (0 degrees longitude) with 357 other longitudes as possibilities. The remaining members (Joplin and Cobain) died within 2 degrees of the 120th degree West Meridian! There are obviously great odds against 4 BIG SIX members dying within 2 degrees of the Prime Meridian, and the other 2 members dying within 2 degrees of the 120th degree West Meridian. There are over 350 other eligible degrees of longitude to mark occurrences of death and the BIG SIX only have these two densely concentrated ranges of longitude for their pattern. New York City is highly populated and has claimed the lives of multiple performers, but none of the BIG SIX died within 2,000 miles of the U.S. East Coast!

DEATH LONGITUDE

CITY, STATE, COUNTRY

WINEHOUSE WAS BORN AND DIED IN THE SAME CITY (LONDON)

COBAIN WAS BORN AND DIED IN THE SAME STATE (WASHINGTON)

JONES WAS BORN AND DIED IN THE SAME COUNTRY (ENGLAND)

JOPLIN WAS BORN AND DIED IN THE SAME COUNTRY (UNITED STATES)

HENDRIX AND MORRISON WERE BORN IN THE UNITED STATES AND

DIED IN ENGLAND AND FRANCE, MAKING THE EXPANSIVE NORTHERN

HEMISPHERE THEIR HUGE COMMON GROUND FOR BIRTH AND DEATH

All BIG SIX deaths occurred near the western coasts of two continents. Another curious note is that while 4 were born in North America and 2 were born in Europe, 2 died in North America and 4 died in Europe. As an aside, Joplin's ashes were spread into the Pacific Ocean and Cobain's ashes were spread into the Wishkah River which ultimately empties into the Pacific Ocean on the West Coast of the United States.

WESTERN COASTS

FROM: "TWENTY SEVENDING" © 2013

"Presence on stage, was like the big bang theory
Then a deafening silence, left us weary
Shuttle Challenger, thundering into space
A fireball, done, and the air without a trace"

A huge event other than the deaths of Joplin and Cobain occurred within 2 degrees of the 120 degree West Meridian and PRIOR to Woodstock. The Monterey Pop Festival was held in Monterey, California (122 degrees West, also Cobain's death longitude) from 6/16 through 6/18/1967 (Cobain's birth year). Brian Jones introduced Jimi Hendrix at the festival. "The Rolling Stones" (Brian Jones) reportedly did not play due to work visa difficulties stemming from recent arrests in Europe, and "The Doors" (Jim Morrison) did not play due to a falling out with organizers. Jimi Hendrix played "Wild Thing," for one of his performances. Janis Joplin sang "Ball and Chain" with "Big Brother and the Holding Company," which landed the group a contract with Columbia Records. As with Woodstock 26 months later, Hendrix and Joplin would be the only members of the CORE FOUR to perform at the event.

While Cobain was 2 years old when Woodstock took place, he was only 4 months old during the Monterey Pop Festival and living almost due north in Aberdeen, Washington. Amy Winehouse would not be born for another 16 years after the Monterey Pop Festival.

MONTEREY POP FESTIVAL

FROM: "TWENTY SEVENDING" © 2013

"Every month is with more days than you had years
Every thought of our loss, floats another tear
Pain in your smile, was hidden in your style
Couldn't you have stayed? Been around for a while?"

Two other previously referenced Monterey Pop Festival performers would eventually die at the age of 27. Ron "Pigpen" McKernan performed with "The Grateful Dead" and was found dead at "H"ome on 03/08/1973 due to gastrointestinal hemorrhage from cirrhosis of the liver reportedly caused by his alcohol intake. Al Wilson of "Canned Heat" (who also played at Woodstock as did Hendrix and Joplin) was found dead on 09/03/1970 on a "H"illside in Topanga, California. His death was labeled as accidental acute barbiturate intoxication, and occurred 2 weeks before Hendrix's death and 4 weeks before Joplin's death.

TOPANGA, CALIFORNIA HILLSIDE

<u>FROM: "TWENTY SEVENDING" © 2013</u>

"No doubt you were international treasures
Boosted millions, in proverbial pleasures
In so few years, you were a powerful source
Became our addition, on this cosmic course"

There were four additional Monterey Pop Festival performers who would die young:

Cass Elliot (32) of "The Mamas and the Papas"

Otis Redding (26) "(Sittin' On) The Dock of the Bay"

Keith Moon (32) of "The Who"

Brian Cole (29) of "The Association"

A total of 9 stars (including Jones, Hendrix, and Joplin) , all present at the Monterey Pop Festival, would die young.

MONTEREY POP PERFORMER DEATHS

LENGTH OF LIFE

STAR	DAYS LIVED	
	TOTAL	BEING 27
COBAIN	9,907	45
JONES	9,988	126
MORRISON	10,070	208
JOPLIN	10,121	259
HENDRIX	10,158	296
WINEHOUSE	10,175	313
AVERAGE	10,070	208

A compelling phenomenon involving averages comes into play when considering the lengths of life for the BIG SIX. When a short 27 years is the length of a human life, it becomes worthy of investigating the total number of days each lived. The length of life for someone dying while 27 can be as short as 9,862 days or as long as 10,227 days. The number 27 surfaces again when calculating the most days a 27-year-old can live as 10,227! Another way of looking at the most days any 27-year-old can live is to say one's last day of being 27 totals 10,227 days and the first day of being 28 totals 10,228! Depending on how far a person lives into the 27th year, some will cross the 10,000 day threshold and some will not. Members of the BIG SIX died on both sides of this 5-digit mark.

NUMBER OF DAYS ALIVE

BIG SIX LENGTH OF LIFE COINCIDENCES

Brian Jones   13 days short of exceeding 10,000

Jimi Hendrix   69 days short of being 28; '69 is Jones' year
                     of death

Janis Joplin   missed 96 days of being 27, the transposed
                     number (69) for Hendrix's missed days

Jim Morrison   exact average for all Big 6 at 10,070;
                     '70 being year of death for Joplin & Hendrix

Kurt Cobain   shortest life of all; 45 days being 27

Amy Winehouse   the longest life of all, only 52 days until age 28,
                     and died at 52 degrees N

The last two additions to the BIG SIX bring with them the distinction of the shortest and longest lives. Notably, Kurt Cobain, with the minimum number of letters (10) comprising first and last names lived the LEAST amount of time, dying only 45 days into his 27th year. Brian Jones also has 10 letters in his name and lived the second LEAST amount of time, with only 126 days into his 27th year.

Amy Winehouse, with the GREATEST number of letters (12) comprising first and last names, lived the GREATEST amount of time at 313 days into her 27th year. The number of days she had remaining as a 27-year-old was 52. Her death latitude is 52 North, as well as the death latitude for Hendrix, and the number of years between the first American's birth (Hendrix, 1942), and the last American's death (Cobain, 1994), are all 52.

The number of days Jimi Hendrix had remaining in his 27th year at the time of his death was 69 (Brian Jones year of death). Janis Joplin's remaining number of days was (96). That is Jimi Hendrix's number (69) transposed, or flipped.

DAYS OF 27TH YEAR

FROM: "TWENTY SEVENDING" © 2013

"One score, seven years, fans' faces filled with fears
Brilliant vessel to ashes...then reappears
New constellation at the sound of a horn
Taken from Cancer; reborn to Capricorn"

The average BIG SIX total number of days alive is 10,070.

9988+10,158+10,121+10,070+9907+10,175 = 60,419 total
60,419 divided by 6 = 10,070

Here is the 70 again, the year of Hendrix's and Joplin's deaths. It is quite a remarkable coincidence that Jim Morrison lived EXACTLY 10,070 DAYS. He could have lived up to 82 days fewer or up to 50 days longer and still have been the fourth to die at 27 which would have changed the average to a number that would not exactly match ANY of the BIG SIX's lengths of life!

LENGTH OF LIFE COINCIDENCES

FROM: "TWENTY SEVENDING" © 2013

"Fifty-four solstices, days or nights lengthen
Ironically, weary thoughts would strengthen
Wandering off, into a fifth dimension
The problems piled up, too many to mention"

Amy Winehouse was a "veteran" 27 when she died, experiencing all four seasons during her 27th year. As a 27-year-old, Kurt Cobain would only live through part of Winter and a brief portion of Spring before he passed away. Brian Jones would see Winter, Spring, and Summer. Janis Joplin, Jimi Hendrix, and Jim Morrison would live through some of all four seasons as 27-year-olds, like Amy Winehouse, but for fewer days. The total number of days the BIG SIX spent being 27 is 1247 (126 + 296 + 259 + 208 + 45 + 313). The average is 208 days (1247 divided by 6) and, once again, sitting at the overall average is Jim Morrison. His total number of days experiencing the age of 27 is the same as the BIG SIX average at 208.

Strikingly, the number 208 has exceptional significance in the history of music. In 1964, "Fabulous" magazine was initially published as a British pop music magazine whose circulation notably grew to 250,000. In 1969, it was retitled, "Fabulous 208" when it struck a deal with "Radio Luxembourg." Where did the 208 factor into this name? This is another place where numbers are interwoven into almost every facet of life. The radio broadcast wavelength of Radio Luxembourg was 208 meters! The very same number as the average days of being 27 for the BIG SIX, and the exact number of days as a 27-year-old for Jim Morrison.

208 DAY AVERAGE

REPEATING DECIMAL PATTERNS

STAR	DAYS BEING 27	DIVIDED BY 27
COBAIN	45	1.666666...
JONES	126	4.666666...
MORRISON	208	7.703703...
JOPLIN	259	9.592592...
HENDRIX	296	10.962962...
WINEHOUSE	313	11.592592...

When the number of days spent as a 27-year-old is divided by 27, all BIG SIX members' data produce a repeating decimal. This means the portion of the answer to the right of the decimal point is a pattern that will repeat itself an infinite number of times. Mathematicians will "round off" the number at a point or use a symbol to designate the infinite characteristic of the answer.

Taking Kurt Cobain as an example, had he survived 54 days of his 27th year, the formula would yield an answer of "2." This is because 54 divided by 27 yields the answer of "2" and there is no fraction remaining as a decimal number. But all BIG SIX members lived for a number of days as 27-year-olds that produce a repeating decimal when divided by 27.

Most numbers divided by 27 produce a repeating decimal. While there are numerous repeating decimal patterns, there is identifiable sharing of these patterns among the BIG SIX. Joplin and Winehouse share an exact duplicate triple digit repeating pattern, being ".592592." Cobain and Jones share the ".666666" pattern. Morrison has an individual ".703703," as does Hendrix with ".962962."

In summary, Joplin and Winehouse have precisely matching three digit repeating decimal patterns. Hendrix has a three digit repeating decimal pattern that does not fully match Joplin and Winehouse but shares a "2" as the third repetitive digit in their patterns. Jones and Cobain share a pattern of unending "6s" which is also the pattern for Joplin's death latitude divided by Jones' death latitude. Morrison has a totally unique pattern that shares NO digits with any other member.

REPEATING
DECIMALS

CELESTIAL SEASON START DATES

(APPROXIMATE)

SPRING EQUINOX   MAR 21st

SUMMER SOLSTICE   JUN 21st

FALL EQUINOX   SEP 23rd

WINTER SOLSTICE   DEC 22nd

IN TERMS OF DAYLIGHT VERSUS DARKNESS:

EQUINOXES - DAY AND NIGHT ARE EQUAL IN LENGTH

WINTER SOLSTICE - SHORTEST DAY, LONGEST NIGHT

SUMMER SOLSTICE - LONGEST DAY, SHORTEST NIGHT

While Global Positioning System devices, compasses, and maps reference locations and directions on Earth, the earlier Zodiac designations reference the relation of Earth to the universe in terms of within which constellation the all-important Sun rose throughout the year (this has changed very gradually over time). For over 3,000 years, the Egyptians considered the Sun to be the God, Ra. The heavens are divided into 360 degrees, similar to longitudes. Twelve sections of 30 degrees make up longitudinal designations known as the Zodiac. While an oversimplification of the process, this is where astrology and astronomy blend.

ASTROLOGY.....
ASTRONOMY

FROM: "TWENTY SEVENDING" © 2013

"The alphabet plus one, then your final tune
Premature rebirth, made you vanish too soon
Zeus and a mortal, had cradled Hercules
Earth and heaven, can't cooperate?...please!"

The reference point for Aries (0 degrees to 30 degrees) was determined at the Vernal (Spring) Equinox otherwise known as the first day of Spring, or about March 21st. Equinox references the lengths of daytime and nighttime as equal periods of light and darkness. This day is celebrated as a day of rebirth. Each additional 30 degrees of the Zodiac's great sphere designates the subsequent sign, and brings the total number of signs to 12, the same number as our calendar months. The Autumnal (Fall) Equinox occurs on approximately September 23rd.

For the Northern Hemisphere, the Summer Solstice occurs on about June 21st and provides the greatest length of daylight as the sun is shining mostly in the northern hemisphere resulting from the tilt of the Earth's rotation. The Winter Solstice occurs on approximately December 22nd and provides the longest night for the Northern Hemisphere as the sun is shining mostly on the Southern Hemisphere. Although they occur on the same days, Solstices in the Southern Hemisphere are the opposite from Northern Hemisphere Solstices (Northern Hemisphere Spring Equinox occurs on the same day as Southern Hemisphere Autumnal, or Fall, Equinox and the same for Solstices).

These celestial events are closely approximated with all BIG SIX deaths.

EQUINOX
SOLSTICE

DAYS FROM SOLSTICE OR EQUINOX WHEN DEATH OCCURRED

SUMMER SOLSTICE

MORRISON	12 DAYS AFTER
JONES	12 DAYS AFTER
WINEHOUSE	32 DAYS AFTER

SPRING EQUINOX

COBAIN	16 DAYS AFTER

FALL EQUINOX

HENDRIX	5 DAYS BEFORE
JOPLIN	11 DAYS AFTER

Jimi Hendrix died 5 days before and Janis Joplin died 11 days after the FALL Equinox (September 23rd) in 1970. When calculated, this totals 16 days. Kurt Cobain died 16 days after the SPRING Equinox (March 20th) in 1994. Each Equinox (when days and nights are of equal length no matter where you are on Earth) occurs when the direct (perpendicular) rays of the Sun are crossing the Equator. These three artists comprise half of the BIG SIX and all died within 16 days of an Equinox!

WITHIN 16 DAYS OF AN EQUINOX

ALL DIED WITHIN 32 DAYS AFTER SOLSTICE OR 16 DAYS OF AN EQUINOX

MORRISON, JONES, AND WINEHOUSE DIED WITHIN **32 DAYS** FOLLOWING THE SUMMER SOLSTICE

COBAIN DIED **16 DAYS** AFTER THE SPRING EQUINOX

HENDRIX DIED 5 DAYS BEFORE, AND JOPLIN DIED 11 DAYS AFTER THE FALL EQUINOX, TOTALING A **16 DAY** CONTINUOUS PERIOD OF TIME

The other half of the BIG SIX (Jones, Morrison, and Winehouse) died within 32 days following a Summer Solstice. Brian Jones and Jim Morrison each died on the 13th day of Summer in 1969 and 1971 with both Summer Solstices occurring on June 21st. Amy Winehouse died 32 days after the Summer Solstice of 2011 (also June 21st that year). Thus, all 3 died within a 32 day post-solstice window established by Amy Winehouse. A Solstice occurs when the Sun's perpendicular rays strike the Earth's surface as far to the North or South as they ever will during the year. These locations occur in a North-South orientation and are due to the tilt of the Earth's axis. These continual seasonal changes are so slight they are essentially not noticed from day-to-day. June 21st is typically the beginning of Summer where direct rays hit the Earth at 23.5 degrees North latitude, and December 22nd as the beginning of Winter at 23.5 degrees South (for Northern Hemisphere seasons). 23.5 degrees North is known as the Tropic of Cancer, while 23.5 degrees South is known as the Tropic of Capricorn, as the Sun rose amidst these constellations during the corresponding solstices when these names were assigned. The area between these two latitudes is thus called "The Tropics."

WITHIN 32 DAYS OF SUMMER SOLSTICE

64-DAY CELESTIAL GROUPING OF DEATHS

32 DAYS FOLLOWING THE SUMMER SOLSTICE

16 DAYS FOLLOWING THE SPRING EQUINOX

16 DAYS SURROUNDING THE FALL EQUINOX

301 OTHER POSSIBLE DAYS REMAIN IN A YEAR, BUT THE BIG SIX ARE
ONLY FOCUSED NEAR THESE EVENTS

None of the BIG SIX died in proximity to the Winter Solstice. When the 32 days following the Summer Solstice are added to the 16 days surrounding the Fall Equinox and the 16 days following the Spring Equinox, the total span of time-segments on the calendar for which the BIG SIX deaths occurred is 64 days. With 301 other days beyond these patterns for BIG SIX deaths to occur, the groupings are remarkable! Note that Jimi Hendrix is the only BIG SIX member to die just BEFORE one of these seasonal events, and that was 5 days BEFORE what would have been his final Autumnal Equinox. Janis Joplin died 11 days AFTER her final Autumnal Equinox. Brian Jones and Jim Morrison died exactly 12 days AFTER their final Summer Solstices. Kurt Cobain died 16 days AFTER his final Spring Equinox. Doubling Cobain's 16-day post Equinox window, Amy Winehouse passed away 32 days AFTER her final Summer Solstice (recall Amy Winehouse also doubled Kurt Cobain when it comes to number of calendar weeks into the year of their deaths, with 30 versus 15). Amazingly, the time segment total for deaths in relation to an Equinox (32 days) is equal to the time segment total for deaths in relation to a Solstice (32 days).

CELESTIAL
GROUPINGS

SEASONS OF DEATH

SPRING	SUMMER	FALL	WINTER
COBAIN	JONES	JOPLIN	
	WINEHOUSE		
	HENDRIX		
	MORRISON		

As solstices and equinoxes dictate seasons, 4 of the BIG SIX experienced Summer as a season of death. Jones, Morrison, and Winehouse are readily recognized as Summer deaths since these events occurred during July. Hendrix also passed away during Summer as September 18th is 5 days before the Fall Equinox (also known as the Autumnal Equinox). The two BIG SIX members who died beyond the boundaries of Summer are Cobain and Joplin. Kurt died during the Spring and Janis died in the Fall. There were no deaths during Winter for the BIG SIX.

NO WINTER DEATHS

BEGINNING LETTER OF NAME AND
DEATH SEASON PATTERN

NO NAMES BEGIN WITH "J" – SPRING:

KURT COBAIN

FIRST, MIDDLE, OR LAST BEGINS WITH "J" – SUMMER:

BRIAN JONES, JIMI HENDRIX, JIM MORRISON,

AND AMY JADE WINEHOUSE

BOTH FIRST AND LAST NAMES BEGIN WITH "J" – FALL:

JANIS JOPLIN

Again, an additional pattern emerges, and it involves a commonality between season of death and the first letters within names. If there is no "J" at all, the death occurred in Spring as for Kurt Donald Cobain. If there is only one "J" in first, middle, or last name, the death took place during Summer as for Lewis Brian Hopkins "J"ones, "J"ames Douglas Morrison, "J"ames Marshall Hendrix, and Amy "J"ade Winehouse. If there are two "J"s, the death took place during Fall, which is the case with "J"anis Lyn "J"oplin.

Additionally, note all BIG SIX members died between leap years. In fact, the CORE FOUR all died BETWEEN the leap years of 1968 and 1972, occurring from 1969 to 1971. Adding Cobain ('94) and Winehouse ('11) does not change the picture as these were not leap years either. Since the BIG SIX were born in '42 and '43, their births did not coincide with leap years. And since Cobain was born in '67 and Winehouse in '83, no leap year coincides with any birth dates of the BIG SIX.

The list of leap years beginning before any BIG SIX members were born and ending after all BIG SIX members had died are as follows:

'40, '44, '48, '52, '56, '60, '64, '68, '72, '76, '80, '84, '88, '92, '96, '00, '04, '08, '12

NO LEAP YEAR
DEATHS

FROM: "TWENTY SEVENDING" © 2013

"Cubit-and-a-half was the length of your life
A black hole was created, cuts like a knife
Now charting a course, to a new universe
Can more gravity end, this terrible curse?"

Prime numbers resound throughout the numerical coincidences of the 27 CLUB. Simply stated, a prime number is a whole number (does not contain fractions or decimals) greater than 1 that can only be divided by itself and 1 to achieve a whole number as an answer. Here are examples: 12 is not a prime number because 12 divided by 6 equals 2 (and both 2 and 6 are whole numbers). 11 is a prime number because you cannot divide 11 by 2, or 3, or 4, or 5, or 6, or 7, or 8, or 9, or 10 and get a whole number for an answer. 11 divided by 2 equals 5.5. Since 5.5 contains a decimal and each other possibility for dividing 11 provides an answer with a decimal, 11 is a prime number. 11 can only be divided by itself and 1, while providing a whole number answer.

What makes prime numbers special? Nothing much as someone counts to ten. 2, 3, 5, and 7 are prime numbers, so 40% of the numbers from 1 to 10 are prime numbers. Note how 2 is the only EVEN number that is a prime number because all EVEN numbers greater than 2 can be divided by 2 and provide an answer that is a whole number, but is not itself or 1. Counting to 100, only 25% of all numbers are prime numbers. Counting to 1,000, about 17% are prime numbers. The greater the number, the less likely it is a prime number, but no "highest" prime number has ever been found. Overall, prime numbers are less common than other ordinary numbers and are, therefore, more unique.

PRIME NUMBER PATTERNS

FROM: "TWENTY SEVENDING" ©2013

"We ask Astrology, Numerology
We are NOT asking for an apology
Just an explanation, some kind of reason
Why darkness could pick, then your final season?"

Prime also designates the meridian assigned as 0 degrees longitude and functions as the mark from which all other meridians are designated.

Prime includes additional definitions, such as being at a time of greatest success and/or capability in one's life.

Counting down from 27 (which is not a prime number), there are 9 prime numbers. They are 23, 19, 17, 13, 11, 7, 5, 3, and 2.

13 is a prime number and surfaces frequently within the 27 Club. 23 is also a prime number and is the number associated with the day of Amy Winehouse's ultimate fate in July of 2011. There seems to be a Prime Number Pattern associated with the transition from the CORE FOUR to the BIG SIX. This pattern lends itself to a possible prediction for the next incredibly famous musical entertainer to join the 27 CLUB (but hopefully, no one joins). Kurt Cobain dies in 1994, 23 years after Jim Morrison, the last to die from the CORE FOUR in 1971. July 23, 2011, is the day when Amy Jade Winehouse follows suit and passes away 17 years after Kurt Cobain. Additionally, please note Winehouse's "W" happens to be the 23rd letter of the alphabet.

If prime numbers are in play with this pattern, 23 is a prime number and so is 17. In a prime number countdown, 19 is the only number skipped in the process. If this pattern repeats itself, the next member to join will be 27 years old and skip the next prime number, 13, in the countdown for number of years following the 27 CLUB predecessor (Amy Winehouse). This means the event would happen 11 years (the next prime number after skipping 13) following the passing of Amy Winehouse in 2011. This designates the year 2022. This would create a BIG SEVEN.

DESCENDING ALTERNATING PRIME NUMBERS

23   19   **17**   13   **11**

FROM: "TWENTY SEVENDING" © 2013

"Superstars from here and now, make it all last
Be the final grain of sand, falls through the glass
Take the long ride, circle the planet on tour
End TWENTY SEVenDING, be part of the cure"

Since Amy Winehouse died on the 23rd day of the month (and it was 23 years after Kurt Cobain died), the pattern could also possibly include the next potential member passing away on the 17th day of the month since the Amy Winehouse pattern includes the day of the month reflecting the same number as total years since the last BIG SIX death event (Cobain passing away 17 years earlier). This suggests the 17th day of a month in 2022, IF this is the pattern.

Would it also include an occurrence between the dates of 4/5 and 10/4 like the rest of the BIG SIX? Might it be within 16 days of an equinox, or 32 days following a solstice? Will there be a "J" at the beginning of a name? Will the death setting begin with an "H?" Will it occur in a city beginning with "Lo?" Will there be an additional subsequent member, skipping a 7-year prime number interval and occurring on the 5-year mark in 2027, another location for 27 to appear? Could that member be the final member since all superstars born in the 1900s will be 28 years old, or older, from that point onward? This would result in a BIG EIGHT. Will it continue throughout the 2000s?

Only time will tell.

?

BIEBER BEWARE

CHARACTERISTIC	PATTERN
27 YEARS OLD UNTIL 3/1/2022	27 CLUB
FIRST NAME IS JUSTIN	NAMES BEGINNING WITH "J"
"J"USTIN PRECEDES "K"URT)	ALPHABETICAL DOVETAILING
"B"IEBER PRECEDES "C"OBAIN)	ALPHABETICAL DOVETAILING
FATHER (JEREMY JACK)	FAMILY BEGINS NAME WITH "J"
SIBLINGS (JAXON & JAZMYN)	FAMILY BEGINS NAME WITH "J"
BORN IN 1994; YEAR COBAIN DIED	BIG SIX DATE LINKS
BORN A PISCES (JONES & COBAIN)	ZODIAC MATCHING IN CLUB
MARRIED	COBAIN MARRIED WHEN DIED
BORN IN CITY BEGINNING WITH "LO"	50% BIG SIX DIED IN "LO" CITY
BORN 27 MILES FROM WOODSTOCK	27 LINK; MUSIC HISTORY
WILL BE 27 DURING 2022	DESCENDING PRIME NUMBER
BORN BETWEEN LEAP YEARS	NO CLUB LEAP YEAR BIRTHS
NOT BORN DURING SPRING	NO BIG SIX SPRINGTIME BIRTHS
12 LETTERS FIRST + LAST NAMES	MATCHES WINEHOUSE
3/1/1994 AS 3+1+1+9+9+4 = 27	COBAIN/HENDRIX ALSO = 27

For purposes of pattern illustration, consider the case of Justin Bieber, born in 1994. Speculation involving his potential for an early demise began in the 2010s. In fact, there were those who doubted Justin would make it into his twenties. He has been mentioned as a potential candidate for the 27 CLUB for a number of years. More recently there was further tabloid speculation of an early demise during Bieber's battle with Lyme disease. His fans would like to have him around forever. Any deviations from safe behavior are a cause for concern in their lives.

But here's to Justin Bieber living into his eighties like Willie Nelson...that is 27 years, three times over. In the investigation of patterns, one is only able to analyze living Bieber patterns such as birthday, birth zodiac, birthplace, name structure and others within the present. There are also observations that can be made in relation to circumstances of death as to whether they might apply, but currently remain inconclusive. Once Justin Bieber turns 28 on March 1st, 2022, all bets are off for him and the 27 CLUB. Until then, speculation will continue. Who else may be at risk? How might a next member shape 27 CLUB patterns? Could these patterns serve as warnings?

How does Bieber fit into 27 CLUB patterns thus far? By the CLUB's namesake, they all made it into their 27th year as has Bieber. His first name begins with "J," as do names for 5 of the BIG SIX. This "J" immediately precedes the "K" of Kurt in the alphabet, and the "B" of his last name immediately precedes the "C" of Cobain in the alphabet. This reveals an ironclad dovetailing of their initials. Additionally, their middle names both begin with "D." Bieber's middle name is "D"rew and Cobain's middle name is "D"onald. Also consider Jim Morrison's middle name is "D"ouglas. Furthermore, Bieber's father's name is Jeremy Jack Bieber, and Justin's two siblings are Jaxon and Jazmyn, all bearing the "J." Amy Jade Winehouse produced a similar angle with a family member's name as her mother's first name is Janis; yes, spelled the same way as Joplin.

J K
B C

VEILED REFERENCES TO 27

FROM TWENTY SEVENDING © 2013

1. HARD KNOCKS SEALED THE LOCKS; HUNDRED AND EIGHT SEASONS
   (108 divided by 4 seasons in a year designates 27 years)

2. NOT EVEN 400 MOONS THAT SHONE SO BRIGHT
   (400 moons represents lunar months of 30 days, or 12,000 days. A death in the 27th year of life never reaches days numbering beyond the 10,000s)

3. WHO KNEW THE WALL WOULD COME AFTER THE MARATHON?
   (Marathon distance is 26.2 miles, falling short of 27; "wall" is point of exhaustion)

4. ONE SCORE, SEVEN YEARS, FANS' FACES FILLED WITH FEAR
   (One score equals 20, plus 7 is 27)

5. ONLY STAYED AROUND, FOR TWO DOZEN AND THREE
   (2 dozen is 24, plus 3 is 27)

6. THE ALPHABET PLUS ONE, THEN YOUR FINAL TUNE
   (26 letters in the alphabet, plus one is 27)

7. EVERY MONTH IS WITH MORE DAYS THAN YOU HAD YEARS
   (28 days in the shortest month of February and is more than 27)

8. YOU WERE ONLY HERE FOR THREE SHY OF THIRTY
   (27 is three less than 30)

9. CUBIT-AND-A-HALF WAS THE LENGTH OF YOUR LIFE
   (A cubit is an ancient unit of measurement equal to the distance from the elbow to the tip of the longest finger & averaged 18 inches. 18 plus half of 18, or 9, equals 27)

10. FIFTY-FOUR SOLSTICES, DAYS OR NIGHTS LENGTHEN
    (There are two solstices each year, summer and winter. 54 divided by 2 is 27)

11. FORK IN THE ROAD, AT MARKER TWENTY-SEVEN
    (Highway systems utilize distance markers to aid in navigation and directions. The turns one takes will sometimes alter the course of a life significantly)

Bieber's history seems to merge with Cobain's more so than any other. Bieber was born the same year Cobain died (1994). Bieber was born under the Zodiac sign of Pisces, as were Cobain and Jones. Cobain was married at the time of his death and was the only BIG SIX member to leave a spouse behind. Bieber is married.

All BIG SIX were born between leap years and so was Bieber. Strikingly, his birthday (March 1st) is the day AFTER Leap Day (February 29th) every four years! When it is not a leap year, Bieber's birthday is the very next day after Brian Jones' February 28th birthday. Justin was born on a Tuesday like Janis Joplin, avoiding Sunday as did all BIG SIX. He was born during Winter as were Jones, Joplin, and Cobain. Bieber will be 27 during portions of 2021 and 2022 which are not Leap Years. 2022 would fit the descending prime number recurrence pattern of those beyond the CORE FOUR, occurring 11 years after the death of Amy Winehouse.

Bieber was born in a city by the name of London, like Amy Winehouse who was born in London, England. The city of Justin Bieber's birth is London, Ontario, Canada, located at 43 degrees North latitude with '43 being the year Joplin and Morrison were born. Astonishingly, there is a town located 27 miles away from London, Ontario, that bears the name of "Woodstock" which is the name of the festival where so much music history was generated. Although the Woodstock music festival was in New York, the parallels are jaw dropping! Three members of the BIG SIX died in cities that begin with "Lo." Those were Hendrix (London), Joplin (Los Angeles), and Winehouse (London), in that order. Obviously, the latter comparison is between Bieber's birth city and these 27 CLUB member's death cities, but that his birth city bears the same death location name of two BIG SIX members as well as the birth location of one is remarkable. Bieber has also maintained homes near "Lo"s Angeles where Janis Joplin died.

Bieber has 12 letters in his name as does Amy Winehouse. Justin Bieber again mirrors Kurt Cobain by sharing the same birthday sum of 17, as does Jimi Hendrix. Bieber's 3/1/1994 birthday added as 3+1+1+9+9+4 equals 27! The expanded birthday sums are also duplicated at 27 for both Cobain and Hendrix.

If Bieber lives beyond the Winter Solstice on December 21, 2021, but not beyond February, 2022, while fitting the 27 CLUB age criterion, he would be the first BIG SEVEN member to pass away during Winter.

Justin Bieber has reportedly booked a $250,000 flight into space. Perhaps it would be a good idea for Justin to wait until he is at least 28 years old to take his flight. Perhaps he should exercise greater caution in general.

BIEBER BEWARE

27 PROMINENT 27 CLUB PATTERNS

1. Jones and Morrison died during the 27th calendar weeks of their respective death years.

2. Jimi Hendrix was born on the 27th day of his birth month.

3. Janis Joplin died 27 days prior to Halloween.

4. Amy Winehouse's mother, Janis Winehouse, was 27 when Amy was born.

5. Hendrix and Joplin died only 16 days apart during the calendar year between Jones'/Morrison's deaths.

6. Jones and Morrison died on the 13th day of Summer exactly 2 years apart to the day.

7. 13 days before exceeding his 10,000th day of life, Brian Jones died.

8. 13 years after Janis Joplin's death, Amy Winehouse was born.

9. 13 weeks separate Joplin's and Jones'/Morrison's death anniversaries.

10. 13 weeks separate Cobain's and Jones'/Morrison's death anniversaries.

11. 13 months to the day after Woodstock, Jimi Hendrix died.

12. All BIG SIX have settings of death beginning with "H."

13. All BIG SIX death anniversaries occur between 4/5 and 10/4—a precise one-half year period of time.

14. All BIG SIX would die within 16 days of an Equinox, or 32 days following the Summer Solstice.

15. Of the BIG SIX, 5 have a name beginning with "J," and the sixth with next in alphabet, "K."

16. Of the BIG SIX, 4 died on the 3rd, 4th, or 5th day of the associated month.

17. All CORE FOUR were born during WWII and died during the Vietnam War.

18. No deaths occur on Sundays, during Winter, or within Leap Years.

19. Deaths occur in order of: male, male, female, male, male, female.

20. Males share birth horoscopes; females have individual birth horoscopes.

21. Of the BIG SIX, 3 died under the Zodiac Sign of Cancer.

22. Of the BIG SIX, 3 experienced the divorce of their parents at age 9, making those combined ages 27.

23. Cobain died in the 4th month on the 5th day, 6 years prior to the new millennium.

24. Of the BIG SIX, 5 died within 4 degrees of latitude (48 North to 52 North).

25. All BIG SIX died within 2 degrees of the 0 degree or 120 degree West meridians.

26. Females mark the northernmost and southernmost latitudes of death.

27. Woodstock was held halfway between the death latitudes of Joplin and Morrison.

As an alternative to the descending prime number formula, maybe the pattern will build from the angle of days following a celestial event for those beyond the CORE FOUR. Kurt Cobain left this world 16 days following an Equinox. Amy Winehouse doubled the number of days at 32 following a Solstice. Might a "next" member double again at 64 days following a celestial event, or simply add another 16 days to total 48? Might it be within 32 days of the Winter Solstice?

Multiple patterns in numbers, letters, days, weeks, years, events, and terrestrial, lunar, solar, and universal phenomena are recognizable for the BIG SIX! Certainly, the 27 CLUB is riddled with patterns. As long as time pushes forward and people remain curious, patterns will evolve.

Hopefully, the cryptic pattern has ended. Hopefully, no more 27s die. Was the 27 CLUB simply a matter of numerous unrelated coincidences, or does the existence of the prolific number of patterns and commonalities indicate it could have formed under an undiscovered or paranormal influence??

WHAT DOES YOUR EYE BEHOLD?

As additional samples, the following are noteworthy "Tip of the Iceberg" 27 Trivia:

Mozart was born in January, 1756, on the 27th and died shortly after the premiere of his 27th concerto.

Morrison was enthused by "The Birth of Tragedy," published by Nietzsche at age 27.

Nelson Mandela spent a total of 27 years in prison.

Paul McCartney was 27 the last time all of The Beatles were in a recording studio together.

Michael Jackson's "Thriller" went Platinum 27 times over.

John Lennon received his U.S. Green Card in July of 1975 on the 27th.

When he assassinated president Abraham Lincoln, John Wilkes Booth was 27.

The sun completes one rotation every 27.27 earth days.

The Space Shuttle Columbia completed 27 successful missions before meeting its destruction.

TRIVIA WITH 27

There are multiple captivating books addressing the 27 CLUB with varied approaches, including:

"27: The Legend and Mythology of the 27 Club," by Gene Simmons

"27: A History of the 27 Club through the Lives of Brian Jones, Jimi Hendrix, Janis Joplin, Jim Morrison, Kurt Cobain, and Amy Winehouse," by Howard Sounes

"The 27 Club...Why Age 27 Is Important," by Michael Owen

"The 27s...The Greatest Myth of Rock and Roll," by Eric Segalstad and Josh Hunter

"The Curse of 27: They have three things in common. Talent, fame... and a tragic death, at the age of 27," by Sarah Milne.

OTHER 27 CLUB BOOKS

APPENDIX

(These are a set of modular lyrics that offer a tribute to the death of any or all BIG SIX members, or any star, or group of stars. Each line is composed of 11 syllables, and each of 27 stanzas can be assembled in any combination or number to tailor the message. "TWENTY SEVenDING" is a hybridization of "TWENTY SEVEN" and "ENDING," signifying tragic loss of life at that age).

TWENTY SEVenDING
(Scars of Stars)
(Reborn to Capricorn)
By: Myron J. Tassin, Copyright 2013

Scattered 'round the world, cities were mangled
From the ashes of a war, stars were spangled
Growing into steel from the remains of rust
Rose to the top on an incredible gust

Growing up brought the pains, that growing up brings
Cramping thumbs practiced, on a neck of six strings
Like the astronaut, that started with a kite
On the whim of maybe, you started the flight

Then like never before, a guitar would roar
Anthem from Woodstock, would play forevermore
Took a thriller ride, along the cosmic blues
And left behind stardust, as the only clues

A drag getting old, one had ended his cruise
TWENTY SEVenDING had already made news
Exactly two years, from when the first one fell
The fourth one died, music cried, tolling of the bell

Could it be, they were all, riding on a storm?
Zodiac, looking back, causes for alarm?
Was the Cancer hiding, in Aquarius?
Libra? Leo? Virgo, Sagittarius?

Was it the Vietnam protest, in our streets?
Was it the Bay of Pigs, and a naval fleet?
Upon the line of the Tropic of Cancer?
Should we look in the stars to find the answer?

Come as you are, because no two are the same
Say no to rehab, makes love a losing game
Spring becomes Summer, Summer turns into Fall
How does early Winter, make sense of it all?

So many dedicated stars, so many complicated scars

The sun set too soon, since your dusk never came
Way too much was lost, we want something to blame
Equinox, paradox, what were the reasons?
Hard knocks sealed the locks; hundred and eight seasons

Who knew the wall would come, after the marathon?
A streak of light through the night, and then be gone?
Launched into the heavens, forever from Earth,
TWENTY SEVenDING, so soon after their birth

Not even 400 moons, that shone so bright
Just like a meteor...the rock turns to light
So beautiful and brief, the thrill turns to grief
Beyond a celestial barrier reef

One score, seven years, fans' faces filled with fears
Brilliant vessel to ashes... then reappears
New constellation at the sound of a horn
Taken from Cancer; reborn to Capricorn

We saw such perfection, through the telescope
You criticized yourself, beneath a microscope
Can't see you in daylight, only in the dark
Ringing like a riddle, leaving such a mark

So many dedicated stars, so many complicated scars

Only stayed around, for two dozen and three
Still so very young; couldn't wait to be free?
Love of your fans, it was platinum and gold
Beautiful Borealis, but seems so cold!

Presence on stage, was like the Big Bang Theory
Then a deafening silence, left us weary
Shuttle Challenger, thundering into space
A fireball, done, and the air without a trace

The Alphabet plus one, then your final tune
Premature rebirth, made you vanish too soon
Zeus and a Mortal, had cradled Hercules
Earth, and Heaven, can't cooperate?...Please!

Every month is with more days than you had years
Every thought of our loss, floats another tear
Pain in your smile, was hidden in your style
Couldn't you have stayed; been around for a while?

No doubt, you were international treasures
Boosted millions, in proverbial pleasures
In so few years, you were a powerful source
Became our addiction, on this cosmic course

So many dedicated stars, so many complicated scars

You were only here, for three shy of thirty
Mourning all we lost, like we were done dirty
We hear the songs you sang, but not the ones you sing
No TWENTY SEVenDING, what would you bring?

Cubit-and-a-half was the length of your life
A black hole was created, cuts like a knife
Now charting a course, to a new universe
Can more gravity end, this terrible curse?

Fifty-four solstices, days or nights lengthen
Ironically, weary thoughts would strengthen
Wandering off, into a fifth dimension
The problems piled up, too many to mention

We ask Astrology, Numerology
We are NOT asking for an apology
Just an explanation, some kind of reason
Why darkness could pick, then your final season?

Your passions paid off, from the early stages
Could sing a book, in a couple of pages
Fame that came forth, from Morpheus in a dream
On top of the world, better than it could seem

Things that would lead, to chaos and confusion
And fame and glory, become an intrusion
Rising star, shooting star, star turns into dust
Lost the will, broken still, taken from the lust

So many dedicated stars, so many complicated scars

Fork in the road, at marker twenty-seven
Leave this world now, or wait to go to heaven?
Even a long life, is a short time on Earth
Forever is forever, once you rebirth

Waiting on the next star, now that you're deceased
Seeing you out there, we hope you rest in peace
Some leaving younger, some a little older
Where are these stars? Mother Earth getting colder

Superstars from here and now, make it all last
Be the final grain of sand, falls through the glass
Take the long ride, circle the planet on tour
End TWENTY SEVenDING, be part of the cure

'Cuz all stars born, someday will die
Take your time 'til Capricorn; stay here and fly
Rising stars observe, and learn from stars before
Go the long distance, and perform many more....................

9 780578 307343